All Fall Down

by David Conrad

Content and Reading Adviser: Joan Stewart
Educational Consultant/Literacy Specialist
New York Public Schools

Spyglass BOOKS

COMPASS POINT BOOKS

Minneapolis, Minnesota

Compass Point Books
3722 West 50th Street, #115
Minneapolis, MN 55410

Visit Compass Point Books on the Internet at *www.compasspointbooks.com*
or e-mail your request to *custserv@compasspointbooks.com*

Photographs ©:
Two Coyote Studios/Mary Walker Foley, cover; Visuals Unlimited/Loren Winters, 4; Visuals
Unlimited/Roger Treadwell, 5; PhotoDisc, 6; DigitalVision, 7; Two Coyote Studios/Mary Walker Foley, 8,
9; Stock Montage, 11; Visuals Unlimited/Jay M. Pasachoff, 13; Visuals Unlimited/C. P. George, 15 (moon);
Stock Montage, 15 (Newton); PhotoDisc, 17, 18, 19; Two Coyote Studios/Mary Walker Foley, 20, 21.

Project Manager: Rebecca Weber McEwen
Editor: Jennifer Waters
Photo Researcher: Jennifer Waters
Photo Selectors: Rebecca Weber McEwen and Jennifer Waters
Designer: Mary Walker Foley

Library of Congress Cataloging-in-Publication Data

Conrad, David.
  All fall down / by David Conrad.
     p. cm. -- (Spyglass books)
Includes bibliographical references and index.
  ISBN 0-7565-0224-1
  1. Gravity--Juvenile literature. [1. Gravity.] I. Title. II. Series.
  QC178 .C637 2002
  531'.14--dc21
                                    2001007316

Contents

Crash!

It makes a dropped glass
fall to the floor.
It lets airplanes land.
It keeps bouncing balls
from flying off into space.
It is **gravity**.

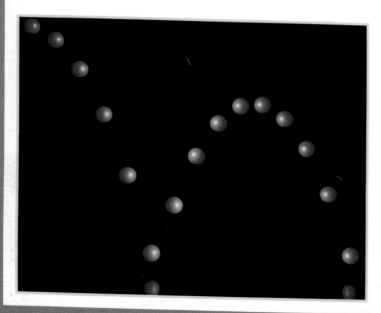

That's a Fact!
Gravity is the weakest *force*
in nature, even though it holds
our *solar system* together.

What Goes Up,
Must Come Down

Gravity can't be seen,
but it is all around you.
When you jump in the air,
gravity slows you down,
and then pulls you back
to the ground.

That's a Fact!
The moon has less gravity than Earth.
On the moon, a person jumping rope
could leap twenty feet in the air!

To see how gravity works,
whirl a ball on a string.
The string is like gravity.
It keeps the ball from
flying away.
If the string breaks,
the ball flies off.

That's a Fact!

If there were no gravity holding you on Earth, you would go flying into space the same way this ball will fly away if the string breaks.

Proving Gravity

More than 2,200 years ago, some very wise men in Greece started to think that there must be a force such as gravity.

That's a Fact!
The Greeks' ideas about gravity were believed for almost 2,000 years!

The Greeks

More than 350 years ago,
a clever man named Galileo
started to study gravity.
He proved that many of
the Greeks' ideas were true.

That's a Fact!
Galileo was put in jail
for saying Earth
went around the sun.
Most people thought
Earth was the center
of everything!

Galileo talking with two other smart men

Less than 100 years after Galileo's work, a man named Sir Isaac Newton proved that gravity was real once and for all.

Some people believe Newton first thought about gravity when an apple fell on his head.

That's a Fact!

Newton saw that the moon had gravity that pulled Earth's water toward it. That is why Earth has *tides*.

Life without Gravity

With no gravity,
there would be no water,
air, plants, or animals.
Nothing would be able
to stay on the ground.
It would all float away.

That's a Fact!
If Earth had more gravity, our bodies would be as flat as pancakes on the ground!

Earth

If Earth had less gravity, it would be cold and dry like the moon.

Imagine how different life would be if Earth had more or less gravity!

Moon

The moon
above Earth

That's a Fact!
All of the air and water have floated
away from the surface of the moon.

Be Stronger Than Earth

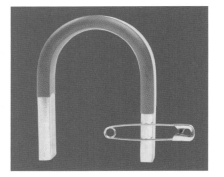

You will need:
- 1 magnet
- 1 safety pin

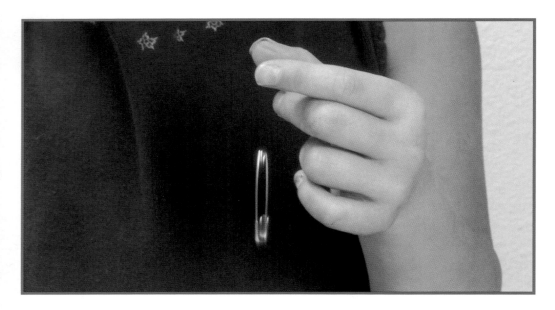

1. Drop a safety pin.
2. Gravity makes it fall.

3. Hold the safety pin
   next to a magnet.
4. Let it go. What happens?

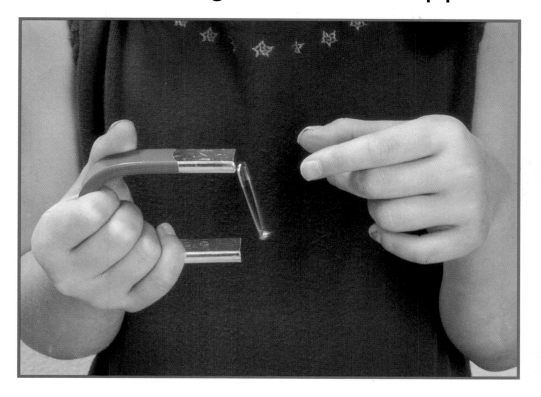

The magnet's power keeps
the safety pin from falling.
It is stronger than gravity!

Glossary

force—a power that causes something to change or move

gravity—the force that pulls all things to one another

solar system—the sun, and the planets (such as Earth) that float around it, held in place by gravity

tides—when gravity makes water get deeper on the side of Earth where the moon is and more shallow on the side away from the moon

Learn More

Books

Murphy, Brian. *Experiment with Movement.* Princeton, N.J.: Two-Can Publishing, 2001.

Riley, Peter. *Forces and Movement.* New York: Franklin Watts, 1998.

Snedden, Robert. *Forces.* Des Plaines, Ill.: Heinemann Library, 1999.

Web Sites

Brain Pop
www.brainpop.com/science/seeall.weml (click on "gravity")

Science Monster
www.sciencemonster.com/gravity_inertia.html

Index

GR: I
Word Count: 206

From David Conrad

I am a scientist who lives in Colorado. I like to climb mountains, square dance, and play with my pet frog, Clyde.